DISCOVERING JOY
IN YOUR CREATIVITY

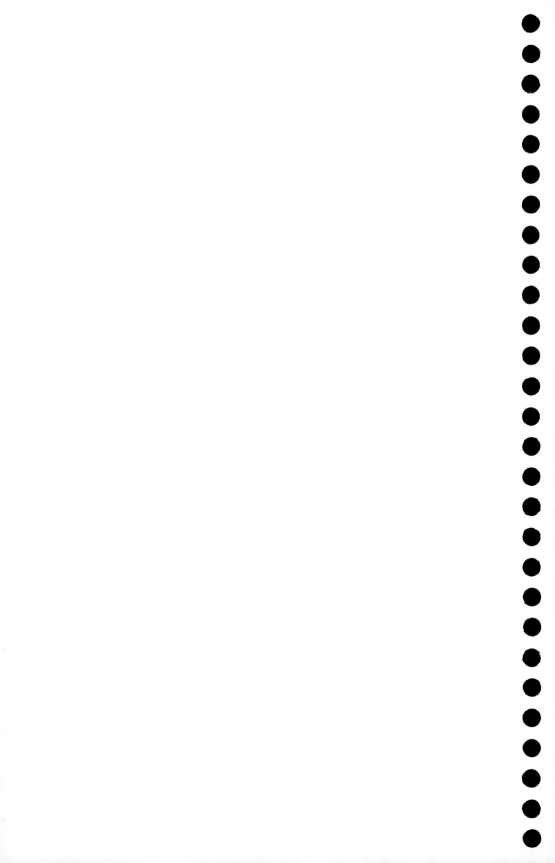

DISCOVERING JOY IN YOUR CREATIVITY

You Are Made in the Image of a Creative God

Margaret Feinberg

Foreword by Luci Swindoll

THOMAS NELSON
Since 1798

NASHVILLE DALLAS MEXICO CITY RIO DE JANEIRO

Published in Nashville, Tennessee, by Thomas Nelson. Thomas Nelson is a trademark of Thomas Nelson, Inc.

Thomas Nelson, Inc., titles may be purchased in bulk for educational, business, fund-raising, or sales promotional use. For information, please e-mail SpecialMarkets@ThomasNelson.com.

Unless otherwise noted, all Scripture quotations are taken from the HOLY BIBLE: NEW INTERNATIONAL VERSION®. © 1973, 1978, 1984 by International Bible Society. Used by permission of Zondervan. All rights reserved.

Scripture quotations marked MSG are taken from *The Message* by Eugene H. Peterson. ©1993, 1994, 1995, 1996, 2000. Used by permission of NavPress Publishing Group. All rights reserved.

ISBN: 978-1-4185-4187-3

Printed in China

10 11 12 13 14 MT 5 4 3 2 1

Contents

Contents

Foreword

Years ago I decided to count the number of artistic projects I could make without ever leaving home. This included all the materials, tools, directions, sketches, and ideas that were actually *in my house*. I wanted to know how long I could create things with only what I had on hand. Would you believe the total came to seven years? I laughed out loud.

In the recesses of my mind, I hear myself saying as a child, "I'm bored, Mama. What can I do?" Without fail, she answered, "Make something with your hands." No doubt she said that because she was capable of making anything with her hands, and often did. I remember a time she gave a bottle of perfume to a friend as a gift. Her friend smiled and said, "Did you make this?" Our family laughed about that for years because it was, indeed, hard to imagine anything my mother couldn't make. Following in her footsteps, I often make gifts for friends. I think the making of a gift is more of a present to me than to the one receiving it. But my friends truly love handmade gifts. I once gave a package to a friend for her birthday, and before she opened it, she asked, "Did you make this?" Knowing I hadn't, I reluctantly said, "Oh, my! What if I didn't?" Without hesitation, she said, "I'll give you another chance." God is the Creator of all things, and we are made in His image. There's great joy in expressing creativity for both the one who gives and the one who receives.

I love this study because everything in it is right up my alley. The topic holds great interest for me, and I love the writing of Margaret Feinberg. She gives suggestions, lists, remedies, questions, and challenging concepts to think about and explore in our own lives. In Margaret's stories you'll often see yourself, but you'll find ways to reach even higher by trying new things in a new way. She starts with the creativity of God but also shows us how to be creative in arts, crafts, business, music, community, gardening, and Bible study. She covers it all, creatively.

Before you dive into this book, read what the apostle Paul has to say about creativity. In Galatians 6:4, he writes, "Make a careful exploration of who you are and the work you have been given, and then sink yourself into that. Don't be impressed with yourself. Don't compare yourself with others. Each of you must take responsibility for doing the creative best you can with your own life" (MSG). That sums it up, doesn't it? Once we sink ourselves into the work we've been given, God will give us ways to express ourselves that are unique to us. And remember, you don't have to be artistic to be creative. Trust me on this—fresh, creative ideas will come, and your life will be filled to the brim with joy.

Maybe you'll even make something with your hands.

—LUCI SWINDOLL

Introduction

Power in Creativity

The initial splash of creativity is displayed in the first words of the Bible: "In the beginning God created. . . ." With those words, God took the plunge into designing the cosmos and the earth. As the first chapters of Genesis reveal, God did not hold back! He created a spectrum of colors, tastes, smells, and sounds.

Today we still enjoy the bounty of all God has made and formed. If you're an early riser, then you know the sunrise is a work of art in and of itself. Some mornings it looks as if God has finger-painted the sky. For those who prefer to sleep in, God makes sure you don't miss His handiwork either, as sunsets reveal colors unimaginable. With vibrant hues of fuchsias, olives, and cerulean blues, God's color spectrum far exceeds that of a Crayola 164-Pack.

This study is designed to douse you in the creativity of God as if it were a cool spring on a hot summer day. My hope is that you'll decide to make time to pull off your shoes and experience the delight that comes with trying something new and unexpected. You may just find yourself refreshed and rejuvenated in ways you never imagined!

We live in a world where we're constantly pressed with demands on every side—from our work, our home, and our families. While many of those requirements are good, if they stack up too high, they can squeeze the life and the creativity out of us. We can become too busy and even too exhausted to engage in our creative pursuits. But that was never what God intended. God wants us to think creatively and express our love for Him and others creatively.

My hope and prayer is that through this study you will once again become awestruck by the Creator of the universe and all He has done and is continuing to do through your life. May you unlock your inner creativity in such a way that it makes a tangible difference, not only in your life, but also in the lives of those around you.

Blessings,

Margaret Feinberg

The Color of Creativity

This section will reveal the importance

of creativity—how it is crucial in

Christianity. It will also describe the

ultimate Creator, His influence upon

human creativity, and creativity's

importance in changing the world.

One

Our Wildly Artistic God

*There is about us, if only we have eyes to see, a
creation of such spectacular profusion, spendthrift
richness, and absurd detail, as to make us
catch our breath in astonished wonder.*

MICHAEL MAYNE

Fluttering through the air, glimpses of vibrant orange can be seen
bouncing from limb to petal. The monarch butterfly is best known
for its distinctive coloration of wings: bright orange with black veins
running throughout. If you've ever seen a picture or one in person,
then you know these creatures are mini works of art.

The wonder of their intricate design is found not just in their
appearance, but in their life spans. They live up to a year, but they
don't stay in the same place for long. Distinctively, monarchs mi-
grate up to three thousand miles every winter. They are the only
species of butterfly to do so. Strangely enough, due to their limited
life spans, the butterflies that journey back each spring are the great-
great-grandchildren of those who came the winter before, yet they

still manage to find their way back to the exact same tree in which their ancestors lived. These inherent details about the monarch butterfly reflect the vast creativity and innovation of our God.

Now take a look around you. The artistry of God is found not just in butterflies, but in each of us as well. When was the last time you took a minute to notice the intricate design of your own hand? Take a good look at your palm and fingers. Now flip your hand over to see the wonder of your fingernails. Aren't they magnificent works of art? God designed you inside and out!

> *Take a good look at your palm and fingers. Now flip your hand over to see the wonder of your fingernails. Aren't they magnificent works of art? God designed you inside and out!*

He did this with every person on the planet. If you're in a room with others or have photos of loved ones in your wallet, take a moment to notice the intrinsic differences in each and every person, the minor details that make them unique. No two people are alike. Blond hair, brown hair, black hair, red hair—they're all so very different.

Now focus on the eyes. Notice the specks of color in the eyes, including the swirls and concentric circles forming the iris. Ponder the faceted nature of the eye itself. Cornea, retina, pupil, and lense all doing separate but distinct jobs for one purpose. This is just one snapshot of God's creativity, but there's so much more because God is concerned with not just the outside, but the inside too.

Let's go a little deeper. Reflect on the unique personalities of the people in your life. The full range of personality types—from the more introverted, quiet types to the extroverted, outgoing ones—are all made by God. This is just one more glimpse of God's creativity.

Yet God's creativity isn't demonstrated in just what we see, but also in what we experience. Think about the last few meals you ate. Which tastes did you encounter? Think about the sweetness of freshly baked chocolate cake, the sourness of just-squeezed lemon juice, or the salty flavor of potato chips. These are all expressions of God's creativity.

Now, if you can, take a step outside or peek out the window. Notice the colors of the sky and the spectrum of colors in the foliage around you. Listen to the broad range of sounds you hear—some more pleasant than others. This, again, is God's creativity.

God could have created our world in black and white, satisfied our hunger with bland nourishment, and made us all look alike. Instead, He decided to enrich the earth with vibrant colors, sounds, tastes, shapes, and experiences. The creativity we witness is a reflection of who He is. God is beautiful, as are the animals, nature, water, and the people He creates.

1. *Make a list of five of your favorite aspects of creation. What strikes you as beautiful in each one?*

2. *If we're not careful, we can take God's creativity for granted. Are there any aspects of nature that you tend to take for granted? Explain.*

3. *What activities help you take the time to stop and admire God's great creation? What prevents you from engaging in these activities more often?*

Creation is not the main focus of discussion in the book of Genesis, yet Genesis contains some of the most important comments on creation in the entire Old Testament. The wonder of creation is outlined in Genesis 1 and 2. The author details the creation of the earth from the very beginning—from those first words uttered by our magnificent, creative God.

4. *Read through **Genesis 1:1–2:3**. In the space provided, connect the box of the day to what was created on that day, also adding the Scripture references as necessary.*

Day	Event	Scripture
Day 1	Light	Genesis 1:3–5
Day 2		
Day 3		
Day 4		
Day 5		
Day 6		
Day 7		

5. Reread **Genesis 1:27**. Rewrite the phrase "in his own image" in the space below. How does it feel to know God made you in His likeness?

One of the greatest days of creation was the final one when God chose to rest.

6. Reread **Genesis 2:2–3**. Why do you think God created a day of rest?

Rest invites creativity. Often while resting and unplugging from the busy demands of life, our creative juices begin to flow, and our power to create is reenergized. At the same time, creativity can also be exhausting and requires rest in order to refuel with fresh ideas. Thus, creativity and rest can go hand in hand.

7. Does being creative tend to energize or de-energize you?

8. Do you ever feel closer to God when you're being creative? Explain.

God's creativity is demonstrated in many aspects of our lives—in people, nature, and even food! When we reflect on all He has made, we can't help but give Him thanks.

Digging Deeper

Creation is not limited to just what is seen in Genesis. Read **Revelation** 4. Memorize verse 11. Does it surprise you that God is recognized as Creator in the book of Revelation? Why or why not? Do you think God will ever stop creating? Why or why not?

Bonus Activity

Capture a snapshot of God's beauty in nature. Choose an artistic expression you naturally enjoy. Draw. Write. Paint. Sculpt. Photograph. Whatever you choose, go ahead and capture a scene of nature—whether it's a single flower or an entire mountain range. Share your work with fellow participants and describe the activity's significance in your life.

Do It Yourself

Try a creativity exercise. Select five everyday items, such as a tote, a lightbulb, a book, a piece of string, and a glass. Now pass an item around the group and challenge each person to think of a creative use for that item. A tote could become a hat or a piece of home decor! Go ahead and be silly. Get those creative juices flowing.

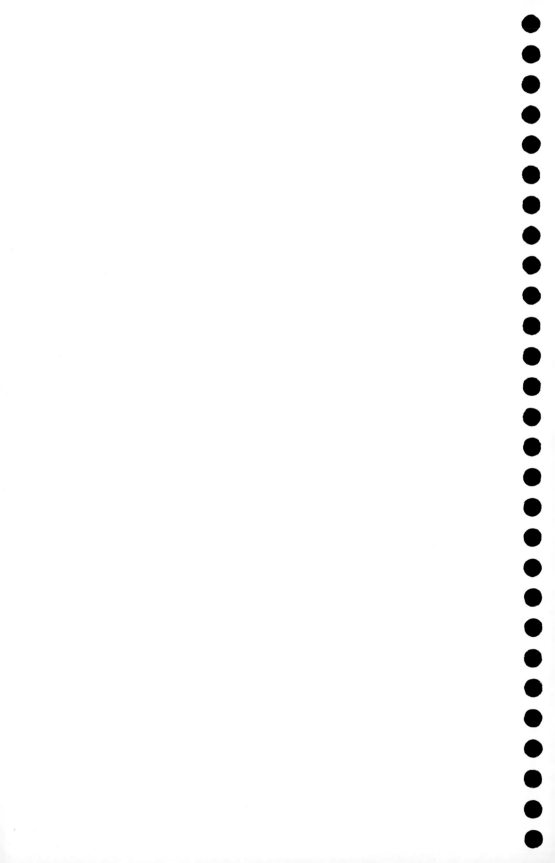

Two

Discovering Your Creative Side

There is a fountain of youth. It is your mind,
your talents, the creativity you bring in your
life and the lives of the people you love.

SOPHIA LOREN

Every day someone somewhere is dreaming about the possibilities of a new business. These people are utilizing their God-given creativity toward developing something fresh and innovative that meets a specific need.

These creative dreamers are located everywhere. For instance, in Philadelphia, a few men are seeing green. Their goal is to make people and businesses environmentally aware. The founders have already convinced one rather large organization to serve all beverages in eco-friendly, corn-based bio-plastic cups. They have also sponsored numerous garden and forest rebuilding projects. These insightful businessmen are converting their aspirations for the world into an enjoyable and unexpected business.

One woman turned her love of dancing into an inventive program for ages one to one hundred. She believes music and dance can teach people creative ways of cooperation with others, as well as self-expression. Her techniques also provide a fun and exciting cardio workout. By expressing her love for dance, this woman has spread that same love to hundreds of others.

Another entrepreneur came up with her innovative idea while pregnant. This soon-to-be-mom wanted a unique way to share the news that she was expecting. Rather than hand her husband a positive pregnancy stick, she decided to create special greeting cards straight from the baby. The cards are representative of what her child might be thinking in the womb, such as "Can't wait to meet you!" or "Counting down the days until I can be spoiled!"

While not every creative idea will launch a new business or job, embracing creativity is an amazing outlet to investigate, discover, examine, and grow.

Sometimes creative opportunities come from the most unlikely encounters. If you've ever driven across the state of Kansas in the fall, you've probably seen a tumbleweed or two. One family decided to harness these dried-out plants to launch a rather unconventional business—they sell tumbleweeds, even Christmas tree tumbleweeds! In fact, NASA is using their tumbleweeds to test the Mars Tumbleweed Rover.

Meanwhile, a couple in Scottsboro, Alabama, developed an idea to start a small business that sells unclaimed baggage left at airports. The store has become a haven for bargain shoppers. From jewelry to clothing, this store sells almost everything you could find in a piece of luggage at a reasonable price. They also donate one-third of everything they receive to charitable organizations.

These are just a handful of examples of people using their God-given creativity to start new businesses and pursue out-of-the-box ideas. While not every creative idea will launch a new business or job, embracing creativity is an amazing outlet to investigate, discover, examine, and grow.

1. *Many people who utilize their creativity ultimately start a part-time business or launch a full-time career. Have you ever pursued a creative idea as a part of your work? What was the response?*

2. *Do you have any creative business or volunteer ideas you've been dreaming about? If so, describe. What's stopping you from pursuing your creative ideas?*

Have you ever noticed how some people live as though life were a Baskin-Robbins ice-cream store? They have all thirty-one flavors mixed together—wild adventures and spur-of-the-moment decisions. There's never a bland moment. On the other hand, there are those who live a life of plain vanilla—playing it safe, never daring to mix in rainbow sprinkles or hot fudge. In the same way, without creativity, our lives would be plain. And while vanilla is a great flavor, it's a whole lot of fun to add in some cookie crumbles and fudge chunks from time to time!

3. What flavors of ice cream would you use to describe your life? Are there any creative additions you'd like to mix in?

Our salvation is a gift of God, and He designed us to do good works to bring Him glory! One of the most valuable and concise summaries of Christianity is found in Ephesians 2.

*4. Read **Ephesians 2:8–10**. Write down the words and phrases in these verses that are the most meaningful to you.*

5. Do you think creativity is involved in the "good works" God has designed you to do? Why or why not? Do you tend to think creatively when it comes to honoring and serving God? Why or why not?

God can use creative people to do all kinds of amazing things! There are numerous examples of this throughout the Bible. One is found in the building of the tabernacle in **Exodus 26–28.** The tabernacle was built as a transferable sanctuary or dwelling place for God as the Israelites roamed the desert led by Moses. This tabernacle described in Exodus later served as a pattern for Jerusalem. Each person involved in building the tabernacle had his own unique contribution to make based on the gifts God had given him.

6. *Read* **Exodus 26:1–29.** *Reflecting on all the specific instructions involved in constructing the tabernacle, make a list in the space below of the various artistic skills needed for its construction.*

One of the most beautiful aspects of the tabernacle is that no one person had all the skills needed to create it. God used people with many different gifts and talents to construct a place for Him to dwell.

7. *Are there any areas in your life in which you're tempted to bury your creative gifts? Explain.*

8. *What changes do you need to make in your life to unleash your creative side?*

> *God created in us a desire to be creative.*
> *We are called to express our creativity and*
> *not bury the talents He has given us.*

Digging Deeper

Read 1 Corinthians 12:12–27. Reflect on your part in the body of Christ. What do you think God has called, created, and gifted you to do that is unique? Why do you think each part of the body is significant?

Bonus Activity

Put your creativity into practice. Select one specific way to live out your inner creativity this week. This can be something as physical as gardening or as relaxing as drawing a picture. Write a song. Craft a poem. Scrapbook old photos. Whatever you choose, pray throughout your experience that God can move to reveal His greater creativity within you.

Do It Yourself

Make a wish list of five activities you really want to do. They could be adventurous, like climbing Mount Everest, or relaxing (but still something you wouldn't normally do!), like sleeping for twelve hours straight. Set aside time this week to complete one of the items on your list.

Three

Creativity Can Make a Big Difference

God creates out of nothing. Therefore, until a man is nothing, God can make nothing out of him.

MARTIN LUTHER

Learning a craft, whether it's scrapbooking, painting, or even shoe-making, can make an immense difference in the world. Need proof? Just ask Blake Mycoskie.

After finishing third in the 2002 season of the television series *Amazing Race*, Blake, a young designer from California, decided to travel to Argentina. While returning to one of his favorite stops, discovered while he was on the show, Blake couldn't help but notice the number of children he saw without shoes.

In many third world countries, walking is the primary method of transportation. Blake soon learned a lack of shoes caused children to receive cuts and scrapes on their feet from the roads. These injuries sometimes took weeks or even months to heal. The wounds allowed the entrance of soil-transmitted parasites into their skin, which ultimately led to infections, and in some cases, amputation. Blake eventually learned of a disease called podoconiosis that results in extreme swelling and deformity in the legs. It is caused by walking or working barefoot in silica-rich soil—common in many rural nations.

He also learned that children were required to wear shoes to attend school. Unfortunately, many children's families were too poor to buy shoes, a fact that closed the door to an education that could have broken the cycle of poverty. All too often, something as simple as the lack of shoes destroys lives through the dangerous possibility of disease, and also the more far-reaching repercussion of the loss of education.

When we recognize the ability to worship God through our creativity, we can fully begin to understand His wondrous creativity.

Blake knew he had to do something. He decided to create the company TOMS. The TOM in TOMS stands for "tomorrow." This company has a unique business model: whenever someone who can afford TOMS shoes buys a pair—whether online or in a department store—one pair is purchased for a child in a third world country. This one-for-one business model is a creative way to involve altruistic people in the support of children in need.

Through Blake's dream, more than 140,000 impoverished children across the world now have shoes on their feet. Even if the kids don't think of their shoes as more than just a better way to win a soccer match with their neighbors, TOMS is making a difference in human health around the world. Blake and TOMS were recently featured in a series of AT&T ads. The thirty-second ads were so popular that AT&T created sixty-second ads. Blake and his company have a new goal of giving away three hundred thousand pairs of shoes in one year.

One man's passion for helping children has led to a fresh, creative, business model that's making a tangible difference in the world. Passions for crafty jobs and hobbies exist within everyone—some more obvious than others. When we recognize the ability to worship God through our creativity, we can fully begin to understand His wondrous creativity.

1. What do you find inspiring about the story of TOMS shoes?

2. If you had seen the same barefoot children whom Blake saw in a third world country, how would you have responded? What do you think prevents us from coming up with creative, innovative solutions to touch people's lives?

God can use any profession to make a difference. Did you know that perfumers, bakers, barbers, boatbuilders, embroiderers, gardeners, needleworkers, sewers, tailors, weavers, molders, and potters are mentioned in the Bible?

3. *Locate each Scripture and, in the space provided, list the unique job(s) outlined in that passage.*

Scripture	Profession(s)
Genesis 11:3	
Exodus 28:3	
Exodus 38:23	
1 Kings 9:26	
Jeremiah 18:1–4	
Jeremiah 37:21	

4. *Does anything surprise you about this list of jobs? Why do you think the Bible includes these types of arts and crafts jobs?*

In the following Scripture, God is compared to being a potter, which is a highly creative profession.

5. *Read Isaiah 64:8. Fill in the sentence below, using your name in the blanks.*

Yet, O LORD, you are our Father. _____ is the clay, you are the potter; _____ is . . . the work of your hand.

6. In what ways do you see yourself as clay in the Potter's hands?

The idea of God constantly shaping us isn't found just in Isaiah; it traces back to the beginning in Genesis. In the creation story, we see God creating out of the soil.

*7. Read **Genesis 2:7**. Do you see any parallels between God as a potter and God creating humankind from the dirt? If so, explain.*

8. Think about your life right now. In what ways is God shaping you to look more like Him?

You may be tempted to think your creative gifts and talents can't make a difference, but God has been using creative people throughout history to bring glory and honor to His name.

Digging Deeper

Read 1 John 4:7–8. God makes it clear that we are supposed to love others. How can you better show love to others? Are there creative ways you can do this?

Bonus Activity

Write a creative poem or prayer. Consider weaving in Scripture or scriptural themes. Try offering up to God what you've written each day. At the end of the week, think about sharing the poem with a friend or your community.

Do It Yourself

Add sparkle to your parties! The next time you are throwing a gathering or dinner party in your home, exercise your creativity by using items you already have to add fun and color. If you need ice, place it in a children's plastic bucket, a small inflatable wading pool, or a large flowerpot. Serve food on paper plates and in bowls that you have decorated yourself. Think outside the box when it comes to displaying food and beverages.

Unleashing Innovation

God has given you—yes, you!—
unique gifts to express yourself
creatively. Your expression won't
look like anyone else's, but that's
the beauty of creativity—it looks
different through every person.

Four

Your Creative Passions

A hunch is creativity trying to tell you something.

Anonymous

Steve and Barb Baker have a great appreciation for music. In fact, they own their own music store. Several years ago, the Bakers learned their son was being stationed in Iraq. Steve was particularly aware of the challenges his son would face, because Steve had served in Vietnam.

Both keenly in love with music, the Bakers wanted to send their son something meaningful that would provide comfort and connect him to home. They sent their son a guitar for his birthday. The instrument became a hit among the troops, and the soldier's friends started asking for their own instruments.

As a result, the Bakers decided to launch Operation Happy Note, an organization that sends out instruments to troops all over the world. Barb devotes herself to making sure everyone who asks for an instrument receives one through donations of musical instruments and funds. With hundreds of people on the waiting list, Barb's job is an important one.

Through the operation, the Bakers have found the instruments have created bonding time for the men and women serving in an unfamiliar country. Rather than the soldiers spending their free time alone and in solitude, the instruments provide them a source of connection, encouragement, and joy. Even in the midst of a challenging situation, the troops are able to sing together and connect through music.

No matter what your interest may be, you just might have the opportunity to make a bigger impact than you ever imagined.

Steve and Barb Baker have received hundreds of e-mails, letters, and visits from soldiers and their families, thanking them for their service to the troops. Who would have thought something as simple as a musical instrument could make such a big difference?

What are you passionate about? Have you ever thought about how your passion could make a difference in the lives of others? Operation Happy Note is a reminder that, no matter what your interest may be, you just might have the opportunity to make a bigger impact than you ever imagined.

1. *What do you enjoy more than anything? If you could do anything on the planet (and every job paid $5 an hour), what would you choose to do?*

Sometimes our creative passion is something we do as a full-time or part-time job. For others, it's a pastime or a hobby. By identifying our creative passions and being willing to explore new options, we unleash change and growth in our lives. Just look at King David. Though he ruled over a nation and kept thousands in his army, he still found time to pen hundreds of songs.

2. Read **Psalm 23** below. Underline or circle all the verbs pertaining to God's working in our lives.

> The LORD is my shepherd, I shall not be in want. He makes me lie down in green pastures, he leads me beside quiet waters, he restores my soul. He guides me in paths of righteousness for his name's sake. Even though I walk through the valley of the shadow of death, I will fear no evil, for you are with me; your rod and your staff, they comfort me. You prepare a table before me in the presence of my enemies. You anoint my head with oil; my cup overflows. Surely goodness and love will follow me all the days of my life, and I will dwell in the house of the LORD forever.

3. Although this is one of the more famous psalms, we can't forget that David wrote these as songs. Do you think David ever guessed that we'd be reflecting on his songs thousands of years later?

4. Do you have a favorite psalm? If so, what is it? Do you have a favorite song or hymn? Why is it so meaningful to you?

When the tabernacle was being constructed, the Bible says the chief architect was a man named Bezalel who was gifted in many creative areas.

5. Read Exodus 35:30–35. According to this passage, what did God do to make Bezalel a great craftsman?

It's interesting to note that God didn't empower Bezalel just to be a talented and gifted workman with the ability to create beautiful works from wood, stone, and metal. God also gave Bezalel a desire to teach.

6. In what ways have you shared the creativity God has given you with others?

7. What stops you from learning and teaching new creative and artistic expressions?

Life is enriched when you embrace your creative side! You can connect to others and God through your unique perspectives, ideas, and expressions.

Digging Deeper

Read Matthew 5:14–16. God tells us that we are the light of the world. How can you utilize your creative passions to be the light to people around you?

Bonus Activity

On a blank sheet of paper, use pictures to record the story of God's activity in your life. You may even choose to add color with markers or crayons. Tell the story of what God has been doing in your life. Then share your pictures with others in your community.

Do It Yourself

As a group, consider a create-your-own-spa afternoon. Choose a time to get together and ask everyone to bring their nail polish, face masks, and scrubbing beads to create your very own spa. Pamper one another and allow time for relaxation and fellowship.

Five

Uncovering Your Resourcefulness

*An essential aspect of creativity
is not being afraid to fail.*

Dr. Edwin Land, founder of Polaroid

You may be in a place where you think you don't have the resources to be creative. That's actually the best possible place to be. If necessity is the mother of invention, then resourcefulness is definitely part of the family. When it comes to creativity, less is more! Sometimes it's easy to get discouraged by what you don't have, but have you ever thought about flipping the situation around and looking for a creative solution?

Pastor Kerry Shook and his wife, Chris, wrote an inspirational book called *One Month to Live,* in which they encourage people to live as if there isn't much time left. By doing so, people can center their attention on their true priorities and how things would change if this scenario were true.

Thousands have taken the thirty-day challenge and had their lives turned upside down—in a good way! One couple completed the challenge together and managed to lose a combined total of one hundred pounds. The husband and wife duo say that they were impacted, not just on the outside, but also on the inside as the thirty-day challenge made them evaluate what's truly important. In the process, they found that their passion for life returned.

Another woman who accepted the thirty-day challenge was going through a personal crisis. She had just been divorced, and her twenty-two-year-old son had tragically died. Through *One Month to Live*, she was empowered to forgive her son's murderer. Another woman also had this challenge hit close to home when her husband was diagnosed with only six weeks to live. Yet during this time the woman and her terminally ill husband learned to live with an unmistakable sense of peace as they trusted God with everything they had.

> *When we are challenged with fewer resources, we often become more creative, innovative, and dependent on God.*

The concept behind *One Month to Live* is something from which we can all learn. Sometimes we think we need to have all the time in the world or unlimited resources in order to start something new or make a change in our lives. But the truth is, when we are challenged with fewer resources, we often become more creative, innovative, and dependent on God. We shift our focus from what we don't have to what we do have; we are in the best possible position to make the most of all those gifts with which we've been entrusted!

1. *What changes would you make in your life if you knew you had only one month to live? What's stopping you from making those changes?*

2. *What relationships would you reconcile or strengthen if you had only one month to live? What's stopping you from making those changes?*

The resources for creativity aren't far out of reach. Newlyweds often develop free and creative date ideas. Stay-at-home moms master budget trimming yet still have five-star fun with their kids. Grandparents discover how to entertain their grandkids with the silliest things. When you focus on what God has given you rather than on what you don't have, God can do great things. Just think of the boy who offered Jesus a few fish and rolls.

3. Read **John 6:1–13**. Do you think the boy ever imagined the small lunch he offered would feed so many? Why or why not? What do you think he told his family and friends after that day?

4. Now put yourself in the shoes of the boy. Do you think you would have had the courage to offer your lunch to Jesus? Why or why not? How would you have felt after seeing this miracle?

5. How does this scenario of the boy and his food relate to your life? Explain.

It's amazing to think what God can do through us when we just make ourselves and our resources available to Him.

6. *Read 1 Kings 17:7–16. Do you think the widow ever imagined her small handful of flour and little jar of oil would last so long? How would you have responded to Elijah?*

This story uncovers an interesting concept—namely, the bowl of flour and the jar of oil would never run empty. They would never be exhausted.

7. *Are you ever afraid that your well of creativity will run dry? Explain. Has your well of creativity ever run dry? What helped replenish it?*

8. *What steps can you take to help keep the well of creativity in your life full?*

> *What we see as lack is often an invitation to be creative. By living each day as if it is our last, we can fully enhance our impact on the world, no matter how limited our resources may seem.*

Digging Deeper

Read **Matthew 6:25–34.** Jesus makes it clear that we're not to worry about anything in our lives, but it's amazing how easy it is to let worries creep into our minds. Reflecting on this passage, what worries tend to distract you from trusting God with everything? What particular words do you find comforting in this passage?

Bonus Activity

For the next thirty days, live as if they are your last days. Consider pairing up with a friend and discussing your experiences. Keep a journal to record how the thirty days are affecting you and your faith.

Do It Yourself

Thinking about redecorating? Trim waste and costs by reusing old furniture instead of purchasing new. Give pieces a fresh look with different-colored paint. Swap furniture between rooms or exchange with a neighbor. You don't have to spend a lot of money to make your home feel new!

Six

Making Time for You

*Time is what we want most, but what, alas, we
use worst, and for which God will surely most
strictly reckon with us when time shall be no more.*

WILLIAM PENN

In the hustle and bustle of daily life, it is rare that we can find time
to be creative. Making time to develop our creative sides can help
strengthen us, energize us, and make life more fun for everyone
around us. Creativity can be incredibly fulfilling.

Ponder these questions: When was the last time you took time to
simply tinker? Explore a new hobby? Join a friend in something she
loves to do? These are all ways in which we can express our creativity, but it does take time.

One company has made creativity a priority. Google's engineers
are given a handful of hours each week just to be creative. They are
encouraged to spend 20 percent of their time working on something
that interests them within a work-related field. By allowing their
employees to get involved in creative jobs that interest them, Google

gives them time to pursue their ideas. This has resulted in incredible innovations, as well as a fantastic work atmosphere.

After September 11, 2001, one of Google's researchers, Krishna Bharat, was visiting multiple Internet sites to keep up with the latest news following the terrorist attacks. Some mornings he would visit anywhere from ten to fifteen different online news outlets to find more information. One day he realized he could design a program to make the task a lot easier.

Krishna, an expert in artificial intelligence, designed a program and e-mailed it around the company as a helpful tool. A fellow employee recognized the possibilities in Krishna's idea. After further development, it was introduced to the world as Google News. If you've ever been on the site's home page, you've probably taken advantage of this helpful feature that provides headlines from around the globe.

When we take time to simply be creative and explore our interests, without pressure to perform or produce, we may just stumble upon amazing results!

When people work on something that interests them, they tend to put more effort into the idea, design, or project. This could be the reason for Google's great innovation. By giving some of their employees the freedom to explore and create, Google has unleashed some innovative ideas. This principle is true not just at the corporate level, but also in everyday life. When we take time to simply be creative and explore our interests, without pressure to perform or produce, we may just stumble upon amazing results!

1. *What inspires you about the story of Google? What percentage of your time do you dedicate to exploring your interests and new ideas?*

2. *Make a list of four priorities in your life. Now make a list of four things you'd really like to do if you had the time. Do you notice any differences? Explain.*

Priorities	Preferences
1.	1.
2.	2.
3.	3.
4.	4.

3. *Spend a few moments reflecting on your lists. How many of your preferences feature a creative outlet? Are there any areas in your life you need to change so you can spend more time on the things you truly enjoy?*

A recent study revealed that our energy levels naturally change throughout the day. In the morning, our recollection and reasoning skills tend to be the strongest, but by midafternoon, we tend to lose our ability to focus. By evening, most of us have lost our capacity for creativity; except, of course, for those who experience late-night moments of brilliance! It's important to pay attention to your peak times of creativity.

4. *What times during your day do you find yourself most awake, mentally and physically? What are some things you could do then, rather than later, to enhance creativity?*

5. *Solitude was very important to Jesus. Read* **Matthew 26:36, 39;** *Mark 14:32, 35; and* **Luke 22:39, 41.** *In the space below, write down what these passages have in common.*

6. *In your own words, how would you define solitude? What is its purpose? Do you enjoy or dislike solitude? Explain.*

7. *On a scale of 1 to 10, how difficult do you find it to respond to Jesus' command to "come with me by yourselves to a quiet place and get some rest" (**Mark 6:31**)? Explain.*

Easy 1—2—3—4—5—6—7—8—9—10 Hard

8. *In what ways does getting alone with God strengthen your faith? When you are one-on-one with God, how do you creatively express worship to Him?*

By taking time to get away and be alone, we can connect with God and give ourselves time to allow our creative passions to flow. We also need to allow time for rest, as it energizes and invigorates our creativity.

Digging Deeper

Read Psalm 102:25–27. What kinds of things will you be a part of creating that will ultimately perish? What kinds of things have eternal value? Where are you spending the majority of your time?

Bonus Activity

Practice meditation with God. Pull away from the stressors of life and spend time in solitude with your Father. This can be anywhere. Take a long bath. Go on a walk. Make time to simply be quiet in your cubicle. Journal your experiences and share with the rest of the group.

Do It Yourself

Have a blast by creating your own board game. Gather family or friends and make up rules to your game. You can blend rules from other board games or just create your own. Consider using the dice, cards, and timers you already have from games you own. Make sure to write down the rules for future times you and your friends want to play.

Embracing the Arts

Sometimes being creative takes you to the very edge of your personal limits. By taking risks and respecting others and the risks they are taking to be creative, we can celebrate and enjoy creativity.

Seven

Celebrating Your Creativity

Christ is not only a remedy for your weariness
and trouble, but he will give you an abundance
of the contrary, joy and delight.

JONATHAN EDWARDS

For some people, it can be hard to celebrate and revel in their accomplishments. For others, it's far easier. Whether you're more reserved or exuberant, there are times you need to go out of your way to celebrate your own creativity, no matter how difficult the situation.

In 1967 Joni did what many students do during the summer: she went swimming. What began as an enjoyable day ended tragically; she was in a diving accident. At seventeen she became a quadriplegic, unable to use her hands or feet. The depression and despair that Joni experienced were impeding as well. She completely lost any will to live. She was angry and frustrated with God. She didn't understand how He could have let this happen.

After months of depression, Joni slowly began to wonder if God was changing her life for the better. She began to renew her faith and accept her fate. During her two years of rehabilitation, Joni learned how to paint and draw by using her mouth and teeth instead of her hands. Today her artwork is sold and collected throughout the world. She learned to celebrate her creativity even though she lacks the capacity to use her hands.

Even in the toughest situations, we can celebrate the creativity God gives us.

For more than forty years, Joni Eareckson Tada has been a source of inspiration to millions. She has shared her story through public speaking, books, and autobiographies. She has become an advocate for the disabled and shared her faith in countless cities. Through the story of Joni's unfortunate accident, thousands of people have been touched and experienced a rekindling of their faith. Joni's story reminds us that, even in the toughest situations, we can celebrate the creativity God gives us.

1. What inspires you about Joni's story?

2. *Have there been times in your own life when you have been tempted to bury your creativity rather than celebrate it? If so, explain.*

In the New Testament, Matthew (or Levi) was a despised tax collector, yet he hosted a celebration in which he shared his faith with those he knew.

3. *Read **Luke 5:27–29**. Fill in the rest of verse 28:*

   "Levi got up, _____ _____ and _____ him."

4. *Matthew then did something even more extravagant. Reread verse 29. What do you think was the purpose of the banquet held by Matthew?*

Sometimes it's easy to think we have to do extraordinary things to share the good news of Jesus in our lives, but the truth is, we can simply be creative with what we already have. We can throw dinner parties for our friends. We can write songs. We can create artwork. There are many ways to share the good news of what God has done in our lives.

5. *What would be your own creative expression to share the good news of what God has done in your life?*

6. *Read **Galatians 5:14** and **James 2:8**. Rewrite each verse below, using your own creative flare to personalize while retaining the sentiment of the passages.*

7. *Do you think you can truly love your neighbor if you don't love yourself? Why or why not? Why is it important to do things that nurture our souls in order to better love others?*

8. How can you show your creativity through loving others?

> *We need to share our creative talents, not bury them!*
> *Although we may not get the response we hope for*
> *or want, we need to celebrate our creative sides.*

Digging Deeper

Read **Colossians 3:12**. With what attributes must we clothe our-selves? By covering ourselves with those characteristics, we can more fully and deeply love others. Reflect on the verse and consider ways in which you can carry those traits with you daily.

Bonus Activity

Think about some people in your life who have yet to find Christ. Consider ways in which you can show them what your faith means to you, much as Matthew did in Luke 5:27–29.

Do It Yourself

Support your local troops. Find a soldier whom you or a friend knows. Write a letter expressing gratitude and encouraging the sol-dier. Consider asking the soldier if there is anything that he or she (or his or her troop) needs and send a care package. Commit to pray for the troops regularly.

Eight

Celebrating Others' Creativity

*Desire joy and thank God for it. Renounce it, if
need be, for other's sake. That's joy beyond joy.*

ROBERT BROWNING

We can develop an eye for indentifying creativity in others. Have you noticed someone who really knows how to decorate? Someone who has launched a successful business? Someone who has developed wildly creative activities for their kids? How about someone who has found potential in an unlikely population, such as prison inmates?

After a tour of a prison with her husband, Catherine Rohr was astonished by the men she saw there. She expected to see a bunch of locked-up men without hope. Instead, she saw people who had worked their way into successful, though illegitimate, businesses. They had more in common with Wall Street executives than she expected. Drug dealers knew a lot about competition, selling products, and risk management—all acquired business skills. Catherine decided to do something to help the inmates use those skills.

Though she had graduated from a top business school in California and worked her way up on Wall Street, she decided to use her degree and experience to found the Prison Entrepreneurship Program (PEP).

Eligible inmates are invited to apply to be a part of PEP, a four-month program designed to give prisoners the help and hope they need to start a legitimate business once they're released from prison. They're encouraged to design a potential business they could launch. Then they develop presentations on their businesses and compete in a two-day business planning competition.

When we help harness others' creativity, we can assist them in developing their God-given strengths.

Upon the inmates' release from prison, the business plans are sent to top MBA advisers and students across the country. Each MBA teams up with an inmate to guide him or her along the path to realization of these plans. With this conceptual feedback from the professionals, ex-inmates are able to build and shape their own businesses.

Since the beginning of PEP in 2004, Rohr has seen fewer than 10 percent of the men she works with return to prison and more than 98 percent find employment. By taking the time to develop the creativity of others, Catherine Rohr has seen hundreds of lives changed and impacted forever.

Sometimes we struggle to see our own creative potential, but it's usually easy to see the creative potential of others. When we help harness others' creativity, we can assist them in developing their God-given strengths. Who knows, maybe someone will come along and help you harness your own creativity!

1. *What inspires you about the story of Catherine Rohr and PEP?*

2. *Why is it important to celebrate stories like Catherine's about people who make a difference through creative programs and ideas?*

3. *Make a list of three problems within your community that need a creative solution.*

Almost every person has a different way he or she prefers to worship God. From singing and serving to dancing and praying, each individual desires to creatively worship in his or her own unique way.

4. Read **Luke 10:38–42**. Mary and Martha decided to worship Jesus in different ways. Martha thought her way was best and became distracted. Rather than celebrate in what Mary was doing, she tried to pull her away. When it comes to creativity, in what ways are you tempted to be like Martha?

5. In what ways can you better celebrate others' creative expressions of worship?

6. *Another form of creative worship is seen in Matthew; however, not everyone appreciated and celebrated this woman's creativity. Read **Matthew 26:6–13**. In what ways are you tempted to be like the disciples in this passage?*

7. *Reflecting on this woman's story, what would be an outrageously generous and creative expression of worship for you?*

8. *As a community, how can you begin celebrating creativity within your group? Could you throw a party? Have a gift exchange? Host an art display in your church?*

When we cultivate creativity, we can celebrate the innovation in others and become encouragers—looking for every opportunity to build others up.

Digging Deeper

Read Luke 6:38. The Bible overflows with expressions of generosity. Why does the Bible tell us to be generous givers? Throughout this week, consider ways in which you can show your generosity to the people in your life.

Bonus Activity

Is there someone in your life who needs a little encouragement? Consider sending the creative people in your life cards or e-mails loaded with a healthy dose of encouragement. Pick up the phone and offer a kind word or even consider sending a text message.

Do It Yourself

Start your own online business. You don't need a ton of money or a thick business plan to start selling things online. Take advantage of sites like ebay.com, craigslist.com, and etsy.com to sell things you have but don't need. Go through your house and collect any antiques or homemade items you're ready to sell. Start an online account at one of these sites and you're ready to go!

Nine

Celebrating Community Creativity

*Find joy in simplicity, self-respect, and
indifference to what lies between virtue and
vice. Love the human race. Follow the divine.*

MARCUS AURELIUS

While volunteering at their church's food pantry and health clinic, a couple had an unusual idea. They noticed that while the warehouse was providing members of the community with much-needed food supplies, they were still limited to giving people canned, boxed, and prepackaged goods. They knew there had to be an alternative that could provide those in need with fresh produce and a healthier diet.

They developed a creative solution. They decided to start the "Garden O' Feedin'." The couple began cultivating the land right around their church (with the permission of the church's leaders, of course!), and planted tomatoes and peppers, along with other vegetables. In their first year, the garden produced $300 worth of vegetables. Since then the garden has continued to grow, develop, and involve more volunteers and people from the local community. Last year the one-third-acre garden produced more than 20,770 pounds of fruit and vegetables and served more than 1,300 families. Today the garden produces a wide variety of fruit and vegetables, including lettuce, melons, and berries, as well as fresh herbs.

The garden is supplying the community with fresh organic vegetables for those in need, as well as for those who don't have a place to grow their own. Anyone can come, participate, and help out. While the garden isn't certified organic, those who manage the land utilize organic compost, fertilizer, and seeds. Plans are in the works to add another one-third of an acre and space for flowers. In addition, the church plans to add a greenhouse to the property. The church's Web site reads, "Volunteers are always welcome. No experience necessary, just a heart to love God's people!"

> *The creativity of one person is powerful. Imagine what a community that embraces creativity can accomplish.*

The Garden O' Feedin' is a reminder that when we think creatively, we can literally transform our communities by looking for opportunities to serve and involve others.

God gave each of us the gift of creativity. When we put our creative minds together to come up with ways to serve others, we naturally create innovative ideas and solutions. The creativity of one person is powerful. Imagine what a community that embraces creativity can accomplish.

1. What inspires you most about the story of the Garden O' Feedin'?

2. *Has your church or community tried anything like the Garden O' Feedin'? What has been the response?*

3. *Have you ever been involved in anything like the Garden O' Feedin'? If so, what was your experience? If not, what has stopped you from getting involved?*

Acts 2 describes a group of people who decided to live differently as followers of Jesus—meeting, worshipping, and eating together in people's houses. At the time, their gatherings were creative and innovative expressions of what it meant to be the church.

4. *Read Acts 2:42–47 below. Circle the activities in which the believers engaged. What are some creative ways you can spend time with fellow followers of Jesus? What kinds of activities can you think of that would make your time of fellowship more fun and enjoyable and lead to spiritual growth?*

   They devoted themselves to the apostles' teaching and to the fellowship, to the breaking of bread and to prayer. Everyone was filled with awe, and many wonders and miraculous signs were done by the apostles. All the believers were together and had everything in common. Selling their possessions and goods, they gave to anyone as he had need. Every day they continued to meet together in the temple courts. They broke bread in their homes and ate together with glad and sincere hearts, praising God and enjoying the favor of all the people. And the Lord added to their number daily those who were being saved.

One of the creative expressions of a community is caring for others. When we choose to reach out and meet the needs of others, we provide a valuable opportunity for members of the community to use their gifts, grow spiritually, and connect on a deeper level.

5. Read Acts 6:1–7. What was the issue that created contention within the church?

6. How was the issue resolved?

7. *Why do you think it is important for a community to be aware of the needs of its members? How aware do you think your community is of the needs of its members? What changes should be made to raise awareness and introduce creative solutions?*

8. *What needs are in your community right now that are not being resolved? What can you do to help meet those needs?*

> *Sometimes the answers to meeting some huge needs are right in our front yards! As people work together to meet the needs of their communities, all kinds of creative ideas emerge, and many can make a big difference.*

Digging Deeper

Read **John 13:12–17.** God desires that we love and serve others, especially in community. How does Jesus reveal His love for His followers in this passage? How can we mirror this attitude and act of service in everyday life?

Bonus Activity

This week, choose a person in your community who needs a little boost. Consider making her a meal, spending quality time with her, helping clean her house, or buying her something she really needs. Pray for them and yourself as you embark on the journey of celebrating your community. Share your experiences with the group.

Do It Yourself

Make a basket of goodies to give to someone who needs it: maybe a friend who is having a personal crisis, an older woman who has been a mentor to you, or even a charity. Go to your neighborhood dollar store or find the discount aisle in the grocery store. Stock up on special gifts, such as lotions, candles, and your favorite goodies. Buy an inexpensive basket. Place everything inside, and you'll have an inexpensive gift made with love.

Creatively Growing Faith

When God gives us the gift of creativity it's not just for us to enjoy, but it's a gift that we can give back to Him. We can use creativity to spice up and spruce up our relationship with God. We can think of creative ways to engage in worship, prayer, studying the Bible, and sharing our faith.

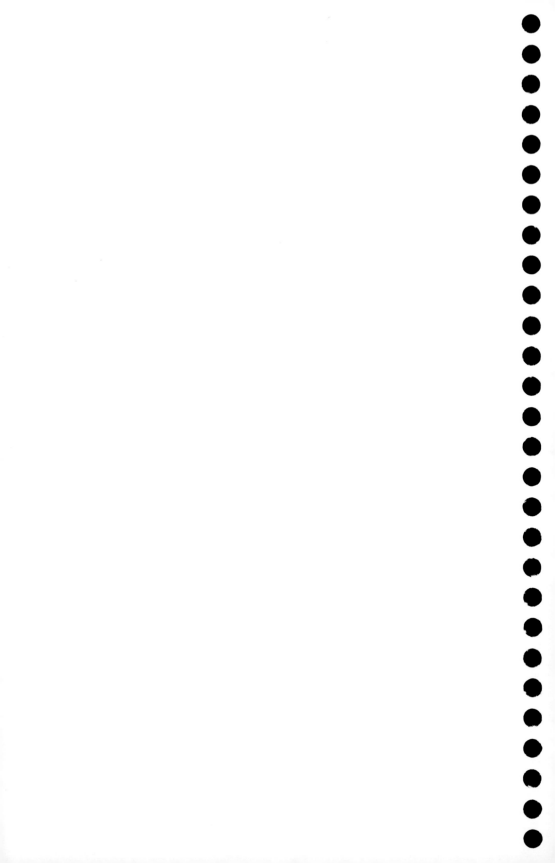

Ten

Knowing God as Never Before

God is continually drawing us to himself
in everything we experience.

GERARD HUGHES

In the fall of 1898, John H. Nicholson was traveling through Boscobel, Wisconsin, and needed a hotel. The place where he stopped was crowded, and he was encouraged to take a bed in a double room with a man named Samuel E. Hill. Over the course of the evening, they discovered that both were Christians, and they shared their evening devotions together.

The next summer the two men met again, along with William J. Knights, and decided to form a ministry for Christian business travelers. They called themselves "Gideons." As the ministry grew, the question arose of how the traveling men could effectively share their faith at the hotels where they spent so much time. It was suggested they supply a Bible for each bedroom in all the hotels in the United States. "The Bible Project" was officially launched in 1908. Shortly after, churches began supporting the movement.

More than one hundred years later, Gideons International has placed more than 1.3 billion Bibles and New Testaments in hotels around the world. The organization's presence can be felt in more than 180 countries. They have distributed Bibles in more than eighty languages.

Who could have imagined what would result from two people staying in a crowded hotel more than a century ago?

The story of Gideon's International is a reminder that God's Word changes people's lives. God's Word is like a megaphone to His people. The Bible is the book in which God has revealed Himself, His ways, and His plans for each of us. Through the Bible, God makes Himself real to us. The Scriptures can challenge us, encourage us, and draw our hearts and lives closer to God.

Yet how often do we open the Bible and find that nothing connects? The reading is dull and distant instead of life-giving and challenging. That's why unleashing our creativity in the context of knowing God can be so powerful. We can jump-start our journeys with God through creativity. We can try new things. We can mix up our daily spiritual routine. And in the process, we may end up encountering God in ways we never imagined!

> *We can jump-start our journeys with God through creativity. We can try new things. We can mix up our daily spiritual routine. And in the process, we may end up encountering God in ways we never imagined!*

1. When is the best time of the day for you to read the Bible?

2. What tends to distract you or keep you from spending more consistent time reading and studying the Scriptures? How do you handle these distractions?

3. What kinds of Bible studies do you enjoy the most? What types of studies really connect you with God's Word in a vibrant, life-giving way? What stops you from engaging in these studies more regularly?

Spending time studying the Bible is amazing because it's a book that never grows old! You can read the same passage a dozen times and still discover something new. What's amazing is, even though the Bible is thousands of years old, it's still as relevant as ever. Why? Because God does not change and human nature does not change. That means as we study, the Bible has a way of providing guidance in life and helping us identify those things that are really important, as well as helping us stay away from self-destructive sinful behaviors and foolish decisions.

4. Read **2 Timothy 3:14–17**. From this passage, make a list in the space below of all the things mentioned that Scripture does in our lives.

Scripture doesn't offer just guidance and instruction; the Word of God also offers protection. It keeps us from making foolish decisions or choosing to settle for less than God's best.

5. Read **Hebrews 4:12–13**. From this passage, make a list in the space below of all the things mentioned that Scripture does in our lives. How have you found this passage to be true in your own life?

6. Read **Matthew 4:1–11**. Why do you think Jesus answered the temptations of the enemy with Scripture? How did the devil respond to Jesus' answers? Have you ever used Scripture to defend yourself from a temptation? If so, describe.

7. *Have you ever had a life-changing encounter with God through the Scriptures? If so, describe.*

8. *What are some creative ways you would like to try to jump-start your spiritual life?*

> *The Bible is like a love letter from God to humanity. The Scriptures reveal volumes about God, His character, and His attributes. We'll never know God as well or as intimately as when we spend time in the Scriptures.*

Digging Deeper

The Bible keeps us from wasting years of our lives on that which does not matter and will not last. Read **Matthew 7:24–27**. Reflect on the passage and the houses described. On which foundation are you building your house today? What are ways you can change that foundation into solid rock?

Bonus Activity

Choose one book of the Bible to read this week. Consider a shorter one such as Philippians or Ephesians. Or consider something a bit longer such as Matthew or Proverbs. Reflect on each verse as you read and pray along the way. Write down how your attitude was altered each day, as well as any truths that were revealed to you. Be sure to share your experiences with the group the next time you meet.

Do It Yourself

Go on a unique vacation! Grab some family or friends and forget the travel agent. Stay local. Go on a "staycation" in a tent in the backyard or at a local hotel. Finding time to get away from everyday stressors can make a huge difference in growing relationships.

Eleven

Growing More Amazing Every Day

Love not what you are, but what you may become.

MIGUEL DE CERVANTES

Eric was a missionary kid. He was born in China to a Protestant missionary family but spent much of his childhood in boarding schools. In 1920 Eric entered the University of Edinburgh where he joined the rugby team. While he loved the sport, he discovered his true athletic talent was running, and he had to make a choice between the two. He chose running and set his eyes on the 1924 Paris Olympics.

When he arrived at the games, he discovered his 100-meter race was scheduled to run on a Sunday. Eric recognized Sunday as the Sabbath and held firmly to the belief that one should honor the Sabbath. His refusal to run meant he was disqualified. The British were particularly disappointed by his decision, but Eric was still determined to run the 400-meter race, a race he hadn't prepared for. On the day of the 400-meter, he ran to victory and set a new world record. Dubbed "the Flying Scotsman," Eric Liddell became an inspiration to many. His refusal to run on Sunday became the basis for the movie *Chariots of Fire*. But the story doesn't stop there. After the Olympics, Eric Liddell followed in his parents' footsteps and worked as a missionary in China for nearly two decades before his death.

Regardless of which gift God has given you, He has great plans for you!

Eric Liddell lived, spoke, ran, and served with a passionate love of God. His story reminds us that no matter what gifts God has given us, we can use them creatively to bring glory to God. Liddell once described feeling God's pleasure when he ran. Many of us have activities in which we feel God's pleasure with our involvement. For some, that activity may be painting or sculpting; for others it may be knitting or quilting; for still others it may be photography or moviemaking. Regardless of which gift God has given you, He has great plans for you!

He wants you to become more amazing every day—to reflect just a little bit more of His image and glory. There's just no telling how far or wide the story of God's goodness may spread because of your gift. Just think of Eric Liddell.

1. *What inspires you most about the story of Eric Liddell?*

2. *Do you think you have to have a story as dramatic as Eric Liddell's in order for God to use you to make a difference in the world? Why or why not?*

3. *Read **John 15:16**. What kind of fruit do you see God growing in your life right now?*

One of the rich lessons from Eric Liddell's life is that he practiced spiritual disciplines. What's a spiritual discipline? It's a simple practice that helps you enrich your relationship with God. For Liddell, that meant keeping the Sabbath. Other spiritual practices include Bible study, prayer, and memorizing Scripture. The Gospels are full of examples of Jesus teaching and practicing disciplines, including solitude, silence, service, fasting, worship, prayer, and fellowship.

4. *Match up the Scripture below to the spiritual discipline described.*

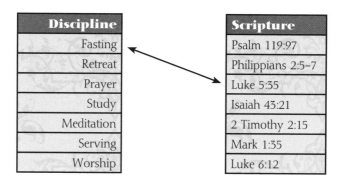

Discipline		Scripture
Fasting		Psalm 119:97
Retreat		Philippians 2:5–7
Prayer		Luke 5:35
Study		Isaiah 43:21
Meditation		2 Timothy 2:15
Serving		Mark 1:35
Worship		Luke 6:12

5. *Reflect on the list of spiritual disciplines above. Which come easily for you? Which are more difficult or challenging?*

6. *What steps can you take to grow in the spiritual practices that don't come as easily to you?*

Growing spiritually means uncorking our creative potential in the ways we engage in spiritual disciplines. Sharing your experiences and journey with God can make a huge impact, not only on your faith, but on others' as well.

7. *Reflecting on the list of spiritual disciplines above, are there any that you'd feel comfortable sharing with someone else? For example, is there someone you'd feel comfortable praying with on a regular basis or committing to serve alongside? In what ways does practicing spiritual disciplines in community make the experience more rewarding or enjoyable?*

8. *In what ways has practicing a spiritual discipline strengthened your own relationship with God?*

*By choosing to do things that are
pleasing to God, we can more fully and
deeply grow in faith and creativity.*

Digging Deeper

Read **Hebrews 10:25.** What does this verse specifically say not to give up on? What are some of the ways in which we can further encourage one another? What people are you encouraging every day? Every week? Every month? Every year?

Bonus Activity

Choose one of the spiritual disciplines described in this chapter. Read more about this practice in the Bible and various other books dedicated to describing and explaining the spiritual disciplines. Choose to practice for one week a discipline that isn't familiar to you. Share your experiences with a friend.

Do It Yourself

Can't sew? No problem—make a blanket! Buy a few yards of fleece fabric from a local craft store in two different colors or designs. Lay one on top of the other. Along each side, make horizontal cuts about four inches long, starting one inch from the top edge of the fleece and working your way down, making cuts about every inch. Double knot the four-inch-long strips together along all of the sides. Enjoy your new blanket.

Twelve

Sharing the Beauty of Your Life

*God's fingers can touch nothing but
to mold it into loveliness.*

GEORGE MACDONALD

In 1957 a woman began planting daffodils. One by one, she placed each bulb into the earth. Today this retired art teacher from California has planted more than one million bulbs. Even though the flowers bloom for only three weeks each spring, many people have enjoyed the beautiful palette of colorful flowers drifting across the almost five acres of land.

Interestingly, the land survived a fire that swept through the area and destroyed the woman's home. Looking out on the charred fields, the woman thought all her hard work had been destroyed. Miraculously, almost all the daffodils bloomed the spring following the fire.

Not only has planting and maintaining the garden been therapeutic for the woman, but she has touched thousands of people who make the pilgrimage to see the garden of daffodils.

Awhile back, a mother and her daughter traveled to the San Bernardino mountain range. As they went along, the daughter became persistent about showing her mother the daffodils. But after a long, tiring walk, the mother was no longer interested in seeing the daffodils. She told her daughter not to worry about the flowers, but the daughter refused to listen.

Eventually, the mother followed the daughter down a path marked "Daffodil Garden." The mother didn't see anything exceptional, but as they turned a corner the fields opened up. It was as if a vat of gold had been poured over the green hills. Sunshine yellows, deep oranges, bright pinks, and pure whites covered the horizon. The flowers were planted in various patterns and designs. Rivers of color flowed and swirled everywhere.

By celebrating beauty in our own lives, others are encouraged and challenged to celebrate it as well.

Astonished and awestruck by the beauty, the mother asked who had taken the time to create such a special garden. The daughter pointed to a lone house in the distance. The mother expressed her wonder over one woman who desired so deeply to share her vision of beauty.

By celebrating beauty in our own lives, others are encouraged and challenged to celebrate it as well. When we live a beautiful life—loving others and God—we can't help but make a lasting impression.

1. What inspires you about the story of the daffodil garden?

2. Toward what would you consider dedicating forty years of your life?

By choosing to love and follow God, we are also choosing to become walking testimonies or stories of what God is doing in our lives. In order to represent Christ, we must decide to imitate Him.

*3. Read **1 Peter 2:1**. Below, list the things that God says must be removed from our lives.*

4. *For most people, it is difficult to remove those things from their lives. Are there specific things in your life that are difficult to release? If so, why?*

5. *Read **1 Peter 2:2–5**. What steps need to be taken to remove all malice and deceit from your life? How can you become a living stone of Christ?*

6. *Read **Colossians 1:9–14**. Below, list the phrases used in this prayer that are most influential for you. Why did you choose these particular phrases?*

7. *Have you considered praying this same prayer for the people in your life? Below, make a list of friends, family members, or strangers for whom you will commit to pray this prayer over the upcoming week.*

8. *In what ways can you allow God to work through you to impact the lives of others?*

> *God is in the midst of creating a masterpiece,*
> *but He isn't done yet. Each of us can use*
> *our creative expressions to share our lives*
> *with others and express our love of God.*

Digging Deeper

God desires us to worship Him in our actions, thoughts, and words. Read **Romans 12:1–2.** How can we offer our bodies over to Christ? What are ways in which we can stop conforming and instead be transformed by the power of God's mercy?

Bonus Activity

If you don't feel ready to share your faith, here are some ways to do so indirectly. Share a special Web site or blog with a nonbeliever. Invite your friends to church or some sort of outreach event. Share a book with a friend. Even if you don't feel comfortable talking directly about your faith, there are ways to share the good news.

Do It Yourself

Are there holidays or birthdays rounding the corner? Do you need an inexpensive way to ship packages? Consider saving money by wrapping gifts inside empty cereal boxes, oatmeal containers, or cookie containers. They come in a variety of sizes and are much cheaper than buying boxes from a store.

Leader's Guide

Chapter 1: Our Wildly Artistic God

Focus: *God's creativity is demonstrated in many aspects of our lives—in people, nature, and even food! When we reflect on all He has made, we can't help but give Him thanks.*

1. *Answers may vary. This icebreaker question is designed to warm up the group to the topic and help participants reflect on the beauty of God's creation. Answers may include, among others: the beauty found in nature (such as mountains or flowers or stars), moments from the Discovery Channel, or items from* National Geographic *magazine.*

2. *Answers may vary. This question is designed to allow readers time to reflect on aspects of nature they may not think about very often— from birds and bugs to plants and forests.*

3. *Answers may vary. Outside activities, such as taking a walk, going on a bike ride, or swimming in the ocean often provide opportunities to stop and admire all that God has done. This question is designed to gently encourage participants to spend more time admiring and enjoying God's creation and thanking Him for all He has created.*

4. *Answers:*

Day	Event	Scripture
Day 1	Light	Genesis 1:3–5
Day 2	Sky and water	Genesis 1:6–8
Day 3	Land and seas; vegetation	Genesis 1:9–13
Day 4	Sun, moon, stars	Genesis 1:14–19
Day 5	Fish and birds	Genesis 1:20–23
Day 6	Animals; man and woman	Genesis 1:24–31
Day 7	Rest	Genesis 2:1–3

5. *Answers may vary but may consist of responses such as intimidating, comforting, or confusing. This question is designed to help readers connect with the reality that God made them and they are a reflection of God.*

6. *Answers may vary, but a day of rest can be encouraging. We are reminded to look at the pace of our lives and remember that all things come from God. Consider having participants read Exodus 20:11.*

7. *Answers will vary, but many people are reenergized by creativity. Although, being creative all the time can be tiring!*

8. *It's not unusual for people to experience the wonder and joy of God's presence when they're using the gifts God has given them.*

Digging Deeper

Answers will vary. Many people associate Revelation with destruction and the end times. God will most likely never stop creating. He is creativity. If He stops creating, we all stop needing creativity.

Chapter 2: Discovering Your Creative Side

Focus: *God created in us a desire to be creative.*
We are called to express our creativity and
not bury the talents He has given us.

1. *Answers may vary. This question is designed to encourage participants to share some of their past activities and business involvements, as well as innovative ideas.*

2. *Answers may vary, but encourage participants to share their innovative ideas and even pursue some of them too.*

3. *Answers will vary but may include descriptions of how an "ice-cream life" looks. As an added activity, encourage each member of the group to draw a picture of their "ice-cream life." What flavor would it be? Why? What does each of the toppings represent? Why?*

4. *The passage reads, "For it is by grace you have been saved, through faith—and this not from yourselves, it is the gift of God—not by works, so that no one can boast. For we are God's workmanship, created in Christ Jesus to do good works, which God prepared in advance for us to do" (Ephesians 2:8–10). Answers may vary but may include such words or phrases as "by grace," "through faith," "not from yourselves," "gift of God," "God's workmanship," and "prepared in advance."*

5. *Answers may vary, but this is an important question. Often when people think about serving God, they think in terms of a very black-and-white list of things to do (or avoid doing), rather than recognizing that God gives us the gift of creativity with which to serve, honor, and worship Him.*

6. *Answers will vary but will include curtain makers, seamstresses, construction workers, woodworkers, and those who could work with gold and silver. There are many different creative talents taken into account in this passage.*

7. *Answers may vary but could include embarrassment or lack of time. This question can reveal many talents that might be unknown to the rest of the group.*

8. *Answers may vary, but challenge participants to make time to be creative and use their creative gifts to honor God and make a difference in the world.*

Digging Deeper

Answers will vary. God has called us all to do different things, yet all are very important things. Have the participants express their creative desires they believe God granted them. Each part of the body works together as one. If one participant enjoys organization and another thrives in stress, those fit together in God's plan.

Chapter 3:
Creativity Can Make a Big Difference

Focus: *You may be tempted to think your creative gifts and talents can't make a difference, but God has been using creative people throughout history to bring glory and honor to His name.*

1. *Answers may vary, but people might be amazed at how something as seemingly minor as having a pair of shoes can make such a positive difference in people's lives.*

2. *Answers may vary.*

3. *Answers:*

Scripture	Profession(s)
Genesis 11:3	Brickmaker
Exodus 28:3	Tailor
Exodus 38:23	Engraver and Embroiderer
1 Kings 9:26	Shipbuilder
Jeremiah 18:1–4	Potter
Jeremiah 37:21	Baker

4. *Even if they seem insignificant, these jobs were crucial in the Bible. Each had its own purpose. The creativity outlined in these professions was utilized by God.*

5. An example of this is "Yet, O LORD, you are our Father. Mary is the clay, you are the potter; Mary is . . . the work of your hand." By having the participants place their names in the blank spaces, they can further relate to God as their Creator. Have each participant read her sentence aloud.

6. Answers may vary, but God is constantly shaping us. We just have to be open to becoming more and more like Him.

7. God formed us from the dust of the ground, just as a potter creates a beautiful sculpture out of mud. This question is designed to emphasize the importance of being created by the ultimate Potter.

8. These answers will vary, but responses may include such things as "responding to my teenager when she talks back to me" or "my relationship with my spouse when we get in an argument over something petty."

Digging Deeper

Answers may vary. People show love to others in various ways. Baking or cleaning for others can show love. Some participants may choose to write a poem for someone, whereas others may choose to make a card.

Chapter 4: Your Creative Passions

> **Focus:** *Life is enriched when you embrace your creative side! You can connect to others and God through your unique perspectives, ideas, and expressions.*

1. *Answers may vary, but participants will be surprised to hear some of the responses. Responses may include being a mom, coaching a team, or cooking. This question is designed to reveal passions that have been tucked away or never given enough consideration.*

2. *The Lord is my shepherd, I shall not be in want. He makes me lie down in green pastures, he leads me beside quiet waters, he restores my soul. He guides me in paths of righteousness for his name's sake. Even though I walk through the valley of the shadow of death, I will fear no evil, for you are with me; your rod and your staff, they comfort me. You prepare a table before me in the presence of my enemies. You anoint my head with oil; my cup overflows. Surely goodness and love will follow me all the days of my life, and I will dwell in the house of the Lord forever.*

3. *Answers will vary, but David probably had no idea the impact his words would have over the years.*

4. *Consider asking participants to read portions of their favorite psalms and share why particular modern songs are so meaningful to them. Gently remind participants that each of these songs is an expression of musical and lyrical creativity.*

5. *God filled him with the Spirit of God and gave him skill, ability, and knowledge in all kinds of crafts. God enabled him to make artistic designs for work in gold, silver, and bronze, to cut and set stones, to work with wood, and to engage in all kinds of artistic craftsmanship. And He gave him the ability to teach others.*

6. *Answers will vary, but this question is designed to encourage participants to share their gifts.*

7. *Answers may include limited time, resources, fear, and lack of knowing how to express oneself creatively. Look for ways to suggest practical and helpful solutions to each one.*

Digging Deeper

We are chosen to go and tell others of the good news of Jesus Christ. Some people might be good speakers, whereas others are good writers. By utilizing our creative passions, we can further God's kingdom.

Chapter 5: Uncovering Your Resourcefulness

Focus: *What we see as lack is often an invitation to be creative. By living each day as if it is our last, we can fully enhance our impact on the world, no matter how limited our resources may seem.*

1. *Answers may vary. Some participants may change everything, whereas some may change nothing. Some might go traveling, whereas some might spend every minute with their families.*

2. *Answers may vary. By having less time, the urgency increases. Encourage the group members to brainstorm about the people they could impact by having this sense of necessity.*

3. *The boy probably never would have guessed, because he had never before seen such a miracle performed. He probably couldn't stop talking about the work Jesus had done to provide the lunch.*

4. *Answers may vary. Participants would probably feel in awe that they had the opportunity to see and be a part of Jesus' miraculous work.*

5. *Answers may vary, but most will relate to the fact that even though it sometimes may seem we don't have much, God gives us the opportunities to utilize our resources and glorify Him.*

6. *Answers may vary. It would have been very scary to have so little food left. The woman said she was planning to die due to a lack of food. Many wouldn't have the faith to believe Elijah, but the woman chose to believe.*

7. *Answers will vary, but even the most artistic people find times when they're completely spent and empty. They need to take time to be filled through various activities and rest.*

8. *Answers may vary. Taking time to be creative, rest, visit an art museum, or spend time with other creative people may be some of the answers.*

Digging Deeper

Answers may vary. Words of comfort include the analogy of the birds or the lilies. God takes care of them, so why can't we trust Him to take care of us?

Chapter 6: Making Time for You

Focus: *By taking time to get away alone, we can connect with God and give ourselves time to allow our creative passions to flow. We also need to allow time for rest, as it energizes and invigorates our creativity.*

1. *Answers may vary. It is inspiring that some companies are allowing time for creativity. Yet often we aren't as gracious or giving with ourselves. All too often, in our fast-paced lives, we don't take time to explore our creative passions.*

2. *Answers will vary. Some examples of things to place on the lists include spouse, kids, extended family, work, personal times, friends, and schooling. Encourage participants to notice any gaps between their general priorities and their preferences.*

3. *Granted, not all time should be focused on yourself, but there should be time each week or month for you to enjoy life and all that God is doing in and through you. Encourage each participant to engage in a favorite activity, whether that's reading a book, gardening, joining a soccer league, or spending more time in prayer. Celebrate the fact that every person needs "me time" and has different expressions of it.*

4. *Every person functions differently. For some, the morning is the easiest time to focus and get the job done, and for others that time is the evening. Encourage participants to choose the time they function best and then spend those hours praying, studying, writing, and creatively thinking.*

5. *Each verse tells of Jesus going off alone to pray.*

6. *Many people will define solitude differently. Consider reading a dictionary definition of the word ("a lonely place; the quality or state of being alone or remote from society; seclusion"). One of the great purposes of solitude is to remove oneself from daily hassles and truly spend time with God. This is easier for some than for others.*

7. *Answers may vary. We all have hectic lives that pull us in every possible direction. Jesus tells us to come away with Him and get rest.*

8. *Answers may vary. In many instances, being alone with God can provide peace and relaxation, as well as spiritual rejuvenation. There are numerous worship experiences, such as singing, praying, reading the Bible, or talking.*

Digging Deeper

Answers will vary. Our salvation and our souls have eternal value. Although everything else we create will eventually perish, we can invest more time in leading others to secure their eternal lives.

Chapter 7: Celebrating Your Creativity

Focus: *We need to share our creative talents, not bury them! Although we may not get the response we hope for or want, we need to celebrate our creative sides.*

1. *Answers may vary. Joni's story is one of hope, encouragement, and inspiration.*

2. *Answers may vary. At one time or another, most of us have been tempted to bury our creative talents because of busyness, fear of rejection, or any one of many other reasons.*

3. *The full sentence should read: "Levi got up, left everything and followed him." Make sure the group understands that Levi was another name for Matthew.*

4. *Matthew had just made a big decision to follow Jesus and leave his life of sin. He wanted a way to share Christ with his friends. He introduced his friends to Jesus.*

5. *Answers may vary. One woman may create a brochure of her testimony and give it to her friends and coworkers. Another may write a poem or create a piece of artwork reflecting her relationship with God. Creativity can be seen in various media.*

6. *Galatians 5:14 reads: "The entire law is summed up in a single command: 'Love your neighbor as yourself.'"*

   James 2:8 reads: "If you really keep the royal law found in Scripture, 'Love your neighbor as yourself,' you are doing right."

7. *Loving others and loving ourselves go hand in hand. If we don't like ourselves, it's hard to like someone else. But if we take care of ourselves and don't run ourselves ragged, we're better able to care for and love others.*

8. *Answers may vary. Each participant may have differing ideas on how to go about loving others through creativity. Creativity can be seen in helping decorate a house, baking something for someone, and even organizing shelves or entire rooms. The goal is to realize that by celebrating our own creativity, we can show love.*

Digging Deeper

We are told to clothe ourselves in compassion, kindness, humility, gentleness, and patience.

Chapter 8: Celebrating Others' Creativity

Focus: *When we cultivate creativity, we can celebrate the innovation in others and become encouragers— looking for every opportunity to build others up.*

1. *Answers may vary. Some women may be shocked that someone took the initiative to make a change in the lives of prison inmates, whereas others may feel slightly intimidated. Rohr has centered her life on celebrating the creativity and innovation of others. This story is very encouraging since it is obvious there is creative potential in every corner of the world.*

2. *Answers may vary. Rohr took a much-overlooked group of people and saw their potential. There could be many people in your life who have overlooked creative potential.*

3. *This question is designed to allow the participants to get their creative juices flowing as they come up with ideas centered on changing the world.*

4. *Answers may vary. Sometimes, like Martha, we can be distracted by service. By thinking everyone should help in the preparations, she forgot the purpose of her service.*

5. *Sometimes appreciating others' creative worship begins by offering people more grace and acceptance. It's also important to recognize that we're all different and that our expressions of worship will be different too.*

6. *The perfume was expensive. It seemed like a waste to break a bottle of perfume just to pour it out. However, the act was a creative way for this woman to worship Jesus. We may be tempted to become overly critical when people spend more or give away more than we think is appropriate.*

7. *Generous and creative worship could be going above and beyond in serving your church or family. Another idea could be giving money to organizations you haven't supported before. There are numerous ways to become a creative and outrageous giver.*

8. *Encourage the group to think of corporate ways they can celebrate creativity.*

Digging Deeper

By becoming generous givers, we can then receive.

Chapter 9: Celebrating Community Creativity

Focus: *Sometimes the answers to meeting some huge needs are right in our front yards! As people work together to meet the needs of their community, all kinds of creative ideas emerge, and many can make a big difference.*

1. Answers will vary but may include the innovative idea, making the most of the church's resources, the involvement of the community, or the number of people fed by the garden.

2. Answers will vary, but encourage participants to share stories of local nonprofits and ministries that are making a difference in the community.

3. Answers will vary, but encourage participants to share stories of past experiences and the reason for any hesitation to become involved in such an endeavor.

4. All too often we think of spending time with fellow believers only in a church setting. While that's healthy, we can spend time at one another's homes, engaging in fun activities like knitting or painting; go on walks together; hike; race cars; or any other kind of enjoyable outlets. Spending time with other believers isn't just about doing church together, it's about doing life together.

5. The Grecian Jews were complaining to the Hebraic Jews because the widows were being overlooked in the daily distribution of food.

6. *The Twelve met together and decided they had two needs: to minister the Word and to care for the widows. They chose seven other men to take care of the widows.*

7. *Answers will vary, but it's important for a community to be aware in order to meet the needs of its members. We all need one another, but sometimes needs go unmet simply because no one is aware of them. Children go without food, single moms go without a much-needed break, couples go without the counseling that would prevent a divorce, all because no one knows of their struggles. A loving, nurturing community will create a safe place for people to share their needs, as well as make contributions from the gifts and resources they have.*

8. *Challenge members to think and speak up about opportunities to serve and bless others. It may be as simple as visiting someone in the hospital, delivering a warm meal to a new mom, buying a tank of gasoline for a single mom, or remembering someone's birthday.*

Digging Deeper

Jesus revealed His love for others by washing their feet. He provided an act of service toward His disciples so they could learn by His example and serve others in the same way. Answers may vary.

Chapter 10: Knowing God as Never Before

Focus: *The Bible is like a love letter from God to humanity. The Scriptures reveal volumes about God, His character, and His attributes. We'll never know God as well or as intimately as when we spend time in the Scriptures.*

1. *Answers will vary, but some will find it best to connect with God first thing in the morning, others during an afternoon break, and still others in the evening before bed.*

2. *This is a crucial question, because many of us face the same distractions every day. When we can identify those distractions, we're in the best possible place to handle them and remove any hindrances from our lives.*

3. *Some participants may prefer reading the Bible or commentaries on their own. Others may enjoy Women of Faith studies or a video-based curriculum. Listen to the different responses and encourage members to engage in studies on their own that help them grow the most.*

4. *Scripture can make us wise for salvation through faith in Jesus Christ; Scripture is useful for teaching, rebuking, correcting, training in righteousness, and equipping us for every good work.*

5. *Scripture is living and active, sharper than any double-edged sword, penetrating and dividing the soul and spirit, joints and marrow. Scripture judges the thoughts and attitudes of the heart. It reminds us that nothing is hidden from God and we will one day give Him an account of our lives. Answers will vary, but encourage participants to share a moment when Scripture really illuminated something in their lives in a profound way.*

6. *Answers will vary, but all of the devil's temptations were based on mistruths. Jesus answered the devil with the truth—God's Word. In the third temptation, it's interesting to note that the devil used Scripture against Jesus, but it was pulled out of context and twisted. Jesus again answered with the truth. After the third temptation, the devil left. Encourage group members to share stories of the power and strength of God's Word in their own lives.*

7. *Answers will vary, but encourage each person to share a powerful moment in her journey with God that was a result of spending time in the Bible.*

8. *Answers will vary, but participants may want to create scrapbooks or prayer books, start journaling, choose a morning of the week to go on a walk and spend time with God, or any number of other activities.*

Digging Deeper

Answers may vary. By choosing to follow Jesus and His words, we are choosing to build our foundation on solid rock.

Chapter 11:
Growing More Amazing Every Day

Focus: *By choosing to do things that are pleasing to God, we can grow more fully and deeply in faith and creativity.*

1. *Answers may vary but may include Eric's conviction and confidence, his willingness to try something new, his dependence on God, or his willingness to sacrifice his own life to encourage and help others.*

2. *Absolutely not! Stories like Eric Liddell's are wonderful sources of inspiration for what God can do through people who are committed to Him. But God does things that are just as amazing through people whose lives aren't featured in movies. By being faithful, loving God, and loving others, we write an inspiring story to everyone who sees our lives.*

3. *Answers will vary, but when you honor God with your life, you can't help but grow fruit in your life.*

4. *Answers:*

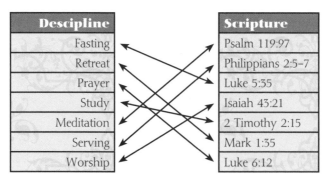

Descipline	Scripture
Fasting	Psalm 119:97
Retreat	Philippians 2:5–7
Prayer	Luke 5:35
Study	Isaiah 43:21
Meditation	2 Timothy 2:15
Serving	Mark 1:35
Worship	Luke 6:12

5. *Answers will vary, but encourage participants to notice that not all spiritual disciplines are easy for everyone. All of them take persistence and, at times, hard work. But they are all incredibly rewarding as we learn more about God and become more like Him.*

6. *It's really important to be intentional and try to learn about practices with which you may be unfamiliar. Consider talking to a spiritual mentor or friend. Read a book. Study what Scripture has to say about that particular topic. Often, we run toward things that come easily but resist the new or unfamiliar. We need to be intentional about growing into all God has for us.*

7. *When we practice our spiritual disciplines alongside someone—even if that person is not in the same room—we often find we provide for each other a sense of accountability, encouragement, and discovery as we share our journeys of growing in God together.*

8. *Encourage participants to share their own stories of how being consistent in a spiritual discipline has led to spiritual growth.*

Digging Deeper

Don't give up on meeting together or encouraging one another. Answers may vary.

Chapter 12: Sharing the Beauty of Your Life

Focus: *God is in the midst of creating a masterpiece, but He isn't done yet. Each of us can use our creative expressions to share our lives with others and express our love of God.*

1. *Answers may vary. The garden represents beauty and serenity. By seeing a garden of that enormity, we would be taken aback. The time and money it took to plant that many flowers was substantial. This woman demonstrated dedication, tenacity, and perseverance.*

2. *Encourage participants to share life passions in which they'd want to spend that much time. A benefit of creating something beautiful and inspiring is that it can often be enjoyed by many.*

3. *Malice, deceit, hypocrisy, envy, and slander are listed within the verse.*

4. *Answers will vary, but each person has different sins that are hard to stop. For some people, it seems impossible to stop being envious. Others find it difficult to stop slandering others.*

5. *This passage says we should crave the spiritual milk, and then we can grow in our salvation. The spiritual milk described here could be the Bible, prayer, or any/all of the spiritual disciplines. By investing our time and our hearts in spiritual practices, we can more fully appreciate and replicate God's will.*

6. *These verses read: "For this reason, since the day we heard about you, we have not stopped praying for you and asking God to fill you with the knowledge of his will through all spiritual wisdom and understanding. And we pray this in order that you may live a life worthy of the Lord and may please him in every way: bearing fruit in every good work, growing in the knowledge of God, being strengthened with all power according to his glorious might so that you may have great endurance and patience, and joyfully giving thanks to the Father, who has qualified you to share in the inheritance of the saints in the kingdom of light. For he has rescued us from the dominion of darkness and brought us into the kingdom of the Son he loves, in whom we have redemption, the forgiveness of sins." Participants may find all of the phrases influential, or a few specific ones may stick out to them.*

7. *Participants may choose only a few close people to pray for or many. This is a question you may want to review next week to see if people prayed and discover if there were any noticeable results.*

8. *Answers may vary, but participants may more readily choose to pray for others or offer to read the Bible or share their testimony with others. By dedicating our lives to Christ, He will provide opportunities for us to share the Good News.*

Digging Deeper

By allowing God to move in us and through us, we can offer ourselves to Christ. By living as Christ asked, we are being transformed by His mercy.

About the Author

Margaret Feinberg is an author and speaker who offers a refreshing perspective on faith and the Bible. She has written more than a dozen books, including *The Organic God* and *God Whispers*. She also wrote the Women of Faith Bible study *Overcoming Fear*. Margaret is a popular speaker at women's events, luncheons, and retreats as well as national conferences, including Catalyst, LeadNow, Fusion, and the National Pastors Conference.

She lives in Lakewood, Colorado, in the shadow of the Rockies, with her six-foot-eight husband, Leif. When she's not writing and traveling, she loves hiking, shopping, blogging, laughing, and drinking skinny vanilla lattes with her girlfriends. But some of her best days are spent communicating with her readers.

So if you want to put a smile on her face, go ahead and write to her!

Margaret@margaretfeinberg.com
www.margaretfeinberg.com
www.margaretfeinberg.blogspot.com

Tag her on Facebook or follow her on Twitter:
www.twitter.com/mafeinberg

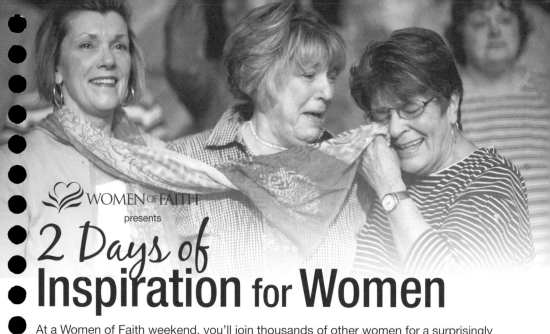

WOMEN OF FAITH

presents

2 Days of
Inspiration for Women

At a Women of Faith weekend, you'll join thousands of other women for a surprisingly intimate, unexpectedly funny, deeply touching 2-day event. Renowned speakers, award-winning musical artists, best-selling authors, drama, and more combine for a hope-filled event like no other.

> " The music was incredible and each speaker's message either brought me to tears, laughing, or both! I have never had a more fulfilling, uplifting experience! You rehabilitated my soul! " *–Debbie*

Coming to a City Near You

Schedule, Talent line up, and more at **womenoffaith.com**
Or call **888.49.FAITH** for details.

Join us at One of These Life-Changing Events!

It's the perfect getaway weekend for you and your friends—or a special time just for you and God to share. **Register Today!**

WOMEN OF FAITH
womenoffaith.com | 888.49.FAITH
Women of Faith events are productions of Thomas Nelson Live Events.

WOMEN OF FAITH®

presents

WOMEN OF FAITH®

WOMEN OF FAITH®
over
the**top**

Two Tours. 29 Cities.
Countless Lives Changed.

Join us at one of these life-changing events!
See when we'll be in your area. Go to **womenoffaith.com** for current
schedule and talent lineup.

Imagine Coming to:

Billings, MT	Denver, CO
April 9–10, 2010	September 24–25, 2010
Las Vegas, NV	**Phoenix, AZ**
April 23–24, 2010	October 1–2, 2010
Omaha, NE	**Portland, OR**
August 13–14, 2010	October 8–9, 2010
Dallas, TX	**San Antonio, TX**
August 20–21, 2010	October 22–23, 2010
Tulsa, OK	**Seattle, WA**
August 27–28, 2010	October 29–30, 2010
Anaheim, CA	**Kansas City, MO**
September 10–11, 2010	November 5–6, 2010
Spokane, WA	**Sacramento, CA**
September 17–18, 2010	November 12–13, 2010

Over the Top Coming to:

Des Moines, IA	Milwaukee, WI
March 12–13, 2010	October 1–2, 2010
Shreveport, LA	**Rochester, NY**
April 23–24, 2010	October 8–9, 2010
Columbus, OH	**Tampa, FL**
April 30–May 1	October 15–16, 2010
Indianapolis, IN	**St. Paul, MN**
August 20–21, 2010	October 22–23, 2010
Washington DC	**Ft. Lauderdale, FL**
August 27–28, 2010	November 5–6, 2010
Philadelphia, PA	**Greensboro, NC**
September 10–11, 2010	November 12–13, 2010
Cleveland, OH	**Hartford, CT**
September 17–18, 2010	November 19–20, 2010
Atlanta (Duluth), GA	
September 24–25, 2010